Mazes

This book belongs to

_____

Beach Toy

Find the toy.

It's in the Bag

Put the bear in the bag.

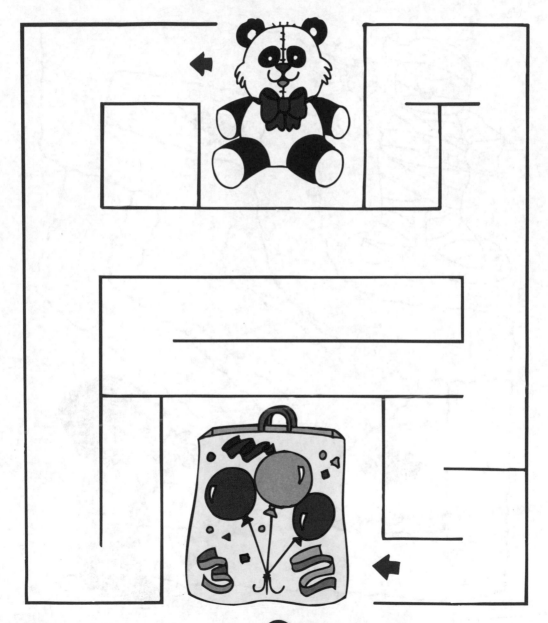

     FS109015 • Mazes

Halloween Friends

Help the friend find his buddy.

Flying Home

Show the bird to its home.

Scarecrows

Help the scarecrow find her friend.

The Chick

Help the chick through the egg.

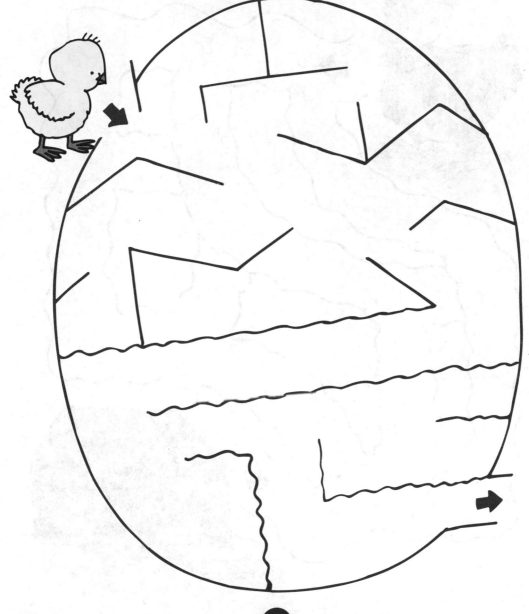

The Henhouse

Find a path to the henhouse.

The Tree

Lead the family to the tree.

Butterflies

Color a path to the flowers.

Owl Friends

Help the owl find his friends.

    FS109015 • Mazes

Time to Eat

Color a path from the bread to the boy.

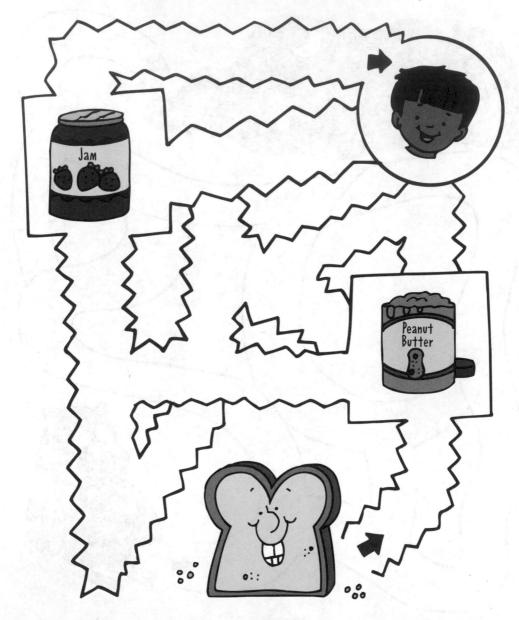

FS109015 • Mazes

Tea Time

Fill the cups with tea.

Top to Bottom

Help the monkey out of the jungle gym.

Popcorn Party

Color a path to the bowl of popcorn.

Sweets

Color a path to the sweets.

    FS109015 • Mazes

Hurry Home

Help the duck find her way home.

17

Camping

Color a path to the camp.

Hide and Seek

Help the pig find her friends.

FS109015 • Mazes

Missing Treats

Find the candy.

FS109015 • Mazes

Let's Sing

Color a path to the music.

    FS109015 · Mazes

Pyramids

Lead the camel to the pyramids.

Lion Tamer

Color a path to the lion.

      FS109015 • Mazes

Hot Soup

Color a path to the pot of soup.

Rainbow Road

Color the road to the rainbow.

25

FS109015 • Mazes

On the Farm

Help the cow to the hay.

Lizard Fun

Help the lizard to the stump.

School Days

Find a way to the school.

Sip! Sip!

Help the mouse to the milk shake.

Breakfast Time

Color a path to the bowl.

Fun at the Park

Color the path to the bottom of the ride.

Jump! Jump!

Help the mouse to the jump rope.

FS109015 • Mazes

Time to Land

Land the balloon.

33

FS109015 • Mazes

Dinosaur Friends

Help the dinosaur find his friend.

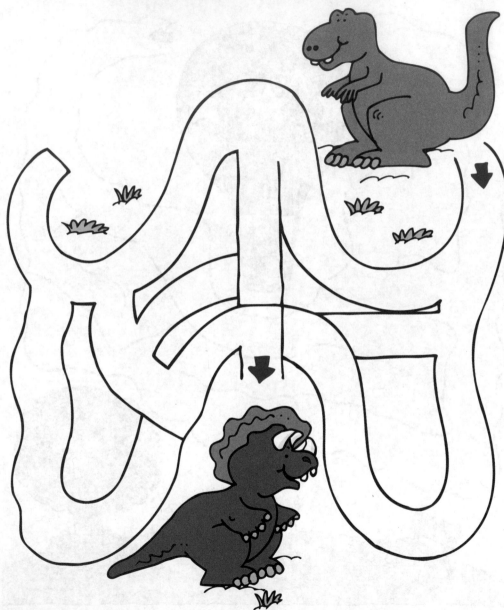

34

Ice Cream

Color a path to the ice cream.

Ho! Ho! Ho!

Lead Santa to his reindeer.

Tractor Trip

Take the tractor to the barn.

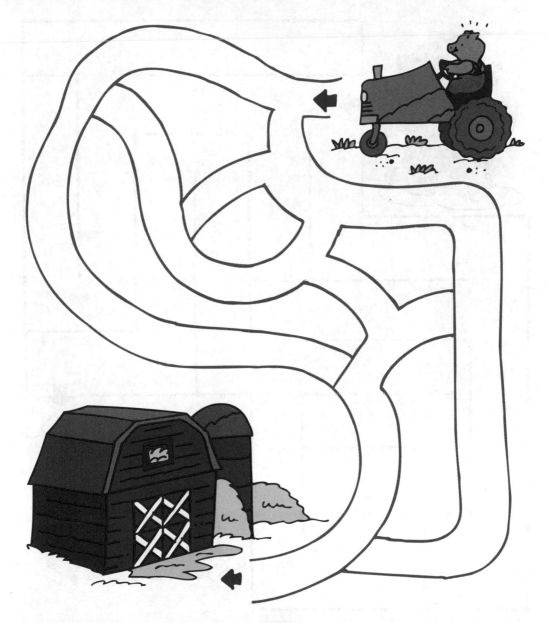

Pin the Tail

Color a path to the lion.

38

FS109015 • Mazes

A Hole in One

Hit the ball into the hole.

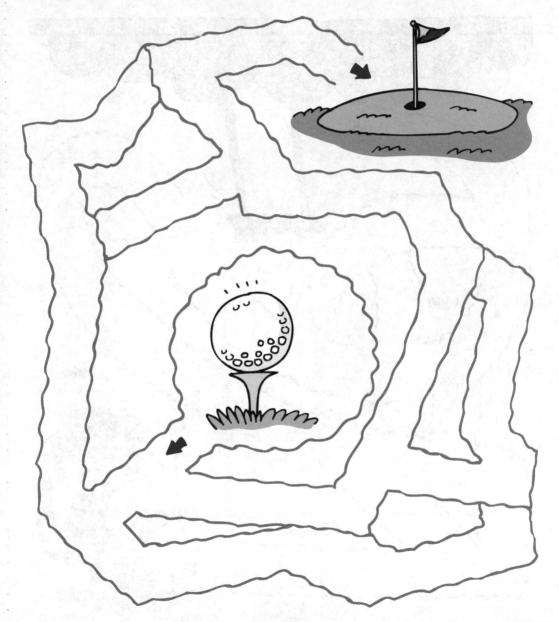

     FS109015 • Mazes

Let's Swing

Color a path to the swing.

Cookies

Color a path to the cookies.

FS109015 • Mazes

Happy Birthday

Help the bunny find her gifts.

Time to Eat

Lead the pig to the corn.

The Bookworm

Color a path through the book.

44   FS109015 • Mazes

To the City

Color a road to the city.

Apple Snack

Color a path to the apple.

46

FS109015 • Mazes

Lost and Found

Find the lost puppy.

Over the Net

Get the ball over the net.

A Dancing Mouse

Color a path to the shoes.

FS109015 • Mazes

Score!

Color a path to the goal.

FS109015 • Mazes

Hungry Horse

Lead the horse to the carrot.

Dirty Dishes

Help clean the dishes.

Sleepy Dog

Color a path to the bed.

On Sale

Color the ☐s to the sale.

Baby's Bedtime

Color a path from **1** to **10** to the baby's bed.

FS109015 • Mazes

_____

is great at doing mazes.

Way to go!

_____
signature

_____
date

FS109015 • Mazes